published in the united states by kaleidoscope kids llc

visit us at www.readkaleidoscope.com

kaleidoscope, *kids bibles reimagined*

library of congress cataloging-in-publication data is available upon request
ISBNs
paperback: 978-1-7360171-6-6
hardback: 978-1-7360171-7-3

cover art by becca godfrey @becca.godfrey
logo design by morgan carter @bymorgancarter
editing by bethany denton @betdenton

To the children and families of
Trinity Tuscaloosa.
Thank you for 10 years of loving
Jesus together.

WELCOME TO KALEIDOSCOPE

First of all, thank you for picking up a copy of Kaleidoscope! We are glad to have you. In the following pages, you'll experience the Bible in a whole new way.

Kaleidoscope was borne from the need to provide a retelling of the Bible for elementary-aged children that is between a "little kid" Bible and an adult translation. In a way, we are the happy medium.

At Kaleidoscope, we are producing single volumes for every book of the Bible. They are designed to read like chapter books, so you'll turn pages and look forward with anticipation to the next volume.

But don't let the fact that we are focused on kids deter you if you are a "big kid!" Good children's books are almost always as good for adults as they are for kids.

Get excited! In the pages that follow, you'll see God's wonderful good news. Our prayer is that his kindness, gentleness, and love will melt our hearts and make us more like Jesus.

The Kaleidoscope Team

From easy-to-understand text to vibrant, beautiful illustrations, *Over the River: The Story of Joshua* accomplishes the same goal as every other Kaleidoscope book on our shelves—it makes the Bible come alive for my kids. Our nightly family devotions will be fueled for weeks with this always-relevant story of obedience, courage, faithfulness, and remembrance. To be honest, it's been years since I've read the book of Joshua from start to finish...I'm just as excited to read as they are!

-Ashlee Gadd, Founder of Coffee + Crumbs

Over The River: The Story of Joshua develops for young readers an exciting adventure story that will match any fiction they may enjoy. This true story, however, not only reveals the mighty deeds of our sovereign God, but continuously points the reader to our Savior, Jesus. What a wonderful resource to offer our families who hope their children will grow into a lifestyle of loving to read the Word!

-Sue Jakes, Children's Ministry Coordinator for the Presbyterian Church in America

There is nothing cooler than seeing your children wake up excited to read and learn the scriptures. Kaleidoscope didn't just teach my kids about the book of Joshua, they helped them apply it to their real life.

-Jerrad Lopes, Founder of Dad Tired

Filled with gorgeous illustrations, this retelling of Joshua will be easily grasped by your elementary-aged child. Ammen beautifully points to Christ throughout this Old Testament book, teaching your child that the truth of the gospel lies within every page of scripture.

-Korrie Johnson, Founder of Good Book Mom - www.goodbookmom.com

"As I've watched my children grow up, I've noticed the gaps in Bible literature, specifically that the distance between Bibles for young children and teens is too large of a gap for most elementary children to leap. That's why I'm thankful for Kaleidoscope and their commitment to chapter-by-chapter paraphrases. In *Over the River*, artful and age-appropriate words ooze with gospel truths that are well-complimented with engaging and sober illustrations."

-Benjamin Vrbicek, local church pastor, author, and father of six children

Finally, a book that doesn't leave out the hard portions of the story of scripture but uses language that is easier for children (and adults) to comprehend. *Over the River* shares the story of Joshua while also keeping the full Bible message in view. *Over the River* has great illustrations for kids and maps! What Bible reader doesn't love a good map?! This is a great book for young readers or for a family read-a-loud.

-Lacey Rabalais, www.laceyrabalais.com

CREATORS

Chris Ammen is the founder of Kaleidoscope and a Children's Pastor. He has a BA and M.Ed. in Elementary Education as well as an M.Div. from Covenant Seminary. When not writing, Chris loves spending time with his wife, Sarah, and their four awesome kiddos!

Marlena Sigman is an artist and designer based in Greenville, South Carolina. She earned a fine arts degree in design at Auburn University, and has a deep love for color, shape, and typography. She finds inspiration in thrift stores, historic buildings, newgrass, and classic literature. If she's not creating art, she's traveling or playing with her dog.

TABLE OF CONTENTS

INTRODUCTION

I remember the summer before middle school like it was yesterday. Certainly, I was not in elementary school because, after all, I was *so* grownup. But I hadn't even spent one minute in a middle school class yet. I was between chapters of my life and there wasn't a great way to describe exactly which chapter I was in.

The book of Joshua is kind of like that summer. It comes after the Pentateuch (the first five books of the Bible, pronounced Pent-a-tuke) and is the beginning of the historical books (which include books like Judges and 2 Kings). Joshua finishes the story of the Pentateuch and begins the story of the historical books.

The Pentateuch goes something like this...

In Genesis 12, God made four crazy promises to an old man named Abraham. He promised to:

> ...bless him so that he would bless others.
> ...give him a great, big family.
> ...give his family a close, covenant relationship with Him.
> ...give his family land to live in.

God came through on His promise and Abraham, against all odds, had a son in his old age, named Isaac. The same promises were repeated to Isaac. Isaac had a son named Jacob. The promises were repeated again to Jacob. Jacob was renamed "Israel" in Genesis 32. Israel had twelve sons and those sons became the heads of the twelve tribes of Israel.

The rest of the Pentateuch is the unlikely story of how Israel wound up trapped in their sin while losing their land as they became slaves under Pharoah in Egypt. God then used Moses to rescue His people and bring them home.

Exodus, Leviticus, Numbers, and Deuteronomy are written about the time of Israel wandering in the wilderness for 40 years on their way back to the land God promised Abraham (otherwise known as the Promised Land).

By the end of the Pentateuch, and the beginning of Joshua, Israel had received most of the promises God made to Abraham: they had been blessed, they were a great nation of many people, and they had a relationship with God. But they were missing one thing...their land.

Getting their land back, however, would be no easy task for three big reasons.

First, the evil Canaanites now lived there.

Second, Moses died.

Third, they had to cross the Jordan River - one of the widest and deepest rivers in the world.

What would Israel do? Would they follow God? Would they ever make it home?

That is where Joshua begins.

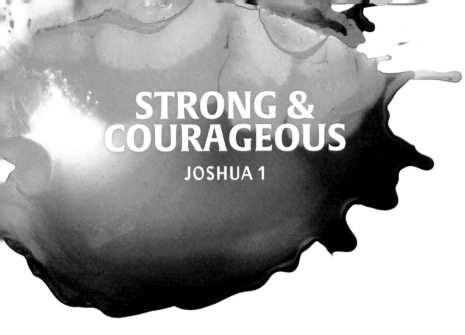

STRONG & COURAGEOUS

JOSHUA 1

The book of Joshua begins with an old dead man, thousands and thousands of people, and a river. But the story of Joshua really began centuries earlier. Here's what I mean...

Many years before, God gave a man named Abraham an incredible promise. Abraham was Joshua's great-great-great (and a lot more "greats") -grandfather. The promise went something like this: Abraham, even though you are 75 years old and your wife is even older than that, you will have many, many children - like, more than all the grains of sand on the seashore. Crazy, right!?

God also gave Abraham a land to live in. This land goes by a few names, but most of the time you'll hear it called the Promised Land.

God kept His promise and gave Abraham children. But his children were not always faithful to God. It's a long story, but eventually, one of Abraham's grandsons, Joseph, was sold by his brothers into slavery a *long* way from home in the country of Egypt.

After hundreds of years of making bricks out of mud and straw, God rescued His people from Egypt. For the next 40 years, Moses led Israel through the desert on their way back to the Promised Land.

Wait!? 40 years!? What took them so long?

Well, you see, that's the point. Sometimes God's people followed His commands and listened. But most of the time, they didn't.

And now, as they made their way to the Jordan River, at the edge of the Promised Land, Moses died.

To add to the problem, the Canaanites, who did not follow God, had built homes and cities and made Israel's land their own. What would God's people do now? Did God have a plan?

Of course, He did! Joshua, who served as Moses's assistant, would become Israel's next leader.

The Lord said to Joshua, "Go over the Jordan River and take the land I have given you. All that I promised to Moses, I now promise to you. Be strong and courageous and be careful to follow all of My commands. Do not turn from them and you will have success wherever you go. Be strong and courageous, for I am with you!"

Joshua then spoke to his officers (the people in charge of the soldiers). "Get everyone ready to cross the Jordan so we can take the land God has given us."

Turning to the tribes of Reuben, Gad, and the half-tribe of Manasseh, Joshua said, "Even though your land is on this side of the Jordan River, you will send your soldiers to conquer the rest of the land on the other side of the river. Once you've won back the land from your enemies, then you can come back and rest." (See Kaleidoscope Corner)

The people answered Joshua, saying, "All that you have commanded us we will do. Wherever you send us, we will go. Just as we obeyed Moses, we will obey you. May the Lord be with you as He was with Moses. Whoever dares to disobey you should be put to death. Be strong and courageous."

Now you should know right from the start that there are two big questions that will shape the entire book of Joshua...

1. Will God's people obey Him? Just because Israel was special to God did not mean they could do whatever they wanted. God knew the best way for them to live was by following His word.
2. Who is fighting the battle? In just a few short chapters, Israel will go to war against the Canaanites. But who is in charge? Israel or God? When Israel allows God to lead, they are victorious. But, when Israel tries to take matters into their own hands and do things their own way, well...things do not go very well at all!

BE STRONG AND COURAGEOUS

Kaleidoscope Corner
The Tribes

It may seem quite strange that God's people were divided into tribes. The Bible doesn't even spend that much time explaining it. Instead, the Bible assumes that the idea of tribes made perfect sense to the first readers. It's sort of like if I talk about D.C. you might immediately think about Washington, D.C., where the White House and Capitol are, without needing much explanation.

Likewise, the story of Jacob (also known as Israel) was so well known at the time that the tribes needed very little explanation. Each tribe came from one of Jacob's sons and was like a smaller family inside of the larger family of Israel.

Jacob's sons came from four different women. From Leah came Reuben, Simeon, Levi, Judah, Issachar, and Zebulun. From Bilhah came Dan and Naphtali. From Zilpah came Gad and Asher. From Rachel came Joseph (who split into two tribes named Manasseh and Ephraim) and Benjamin.

If you follow the story of the Bible all the way to Jesus, something really cool happens with the tribes. Paul, the writer of Galatians, calls those who are "in Christ" the "Israel of God." In Jesus, we have a new kingdom where there are no longer tribes. Instead, people from all tongues, tribes, and nations are one family with God as our Father.

RAHAB

JOSHUA 2

It's quite difficult for thousands of people to cross a river and enter land infested with enemies, all while going unnoticed. So, Joshua decided to send two men on a secret mission of sorts.

"Spy out the land and look closely at the city of Jericho. It's the first city we'll come to and I want to make sure we know what we're up against," Joshua instructed.

The two men did as they were told and crossed the river, entered the Promised Land, and ventured to the impressive, walled-in city of Jericho.

Once in Jericho, the men stayed in the house of a woman named Rahab. Now, you should know that Rahab hadn't lived a perfect life. She broke God's law time and time again by treating more than one man like they were her husband.

News soon traveled to the king of Jericho that spies from Israel had invaded his city. The king sent word to Rahab. "Bring out the Israelites who came to you. They are our enemies!"

What would Rahab do? She could protect the men. But then she risked her own life!

Rahab answered, "Yes, the men did come to me. But I did not know they were Israelites. They have now left and I do not know where they went. Go! Chase after them quickly and you will surely catch them!"

But...that was not exactly the truth.

Instead, Rahab hid the men on her roof underneath stalks of flax while Jericho's soldiers ran towards the Jordan River, hoping to catch the intruders.

Rahab told the spies, "I know the Lord has given you the land. The men of this city and all the surrounding land are afraid of you because they know the Lord is with you. We have heard how the Lord dried up the water of the Red Sea when you came out of Egypt, and what you did to the two kings of the Amorites, Sihon and Og, whom you destroyed before reaching the Jordan River. Our hearts melted because we knew that the Lord, who made the heavens above and the earth below, is your God.

"Please promise that you will protect me and my family as I have protected you."

The men agreed, "Our life for yours...even to death!"

Rahab let the men down from the roof with a long piece of rope, for her house was built into the city wall. In parting, she said, "Go hide in the hills. You will be safe there. After three days, return to your people."

The men replied, "Rahab, you have been so kind to us because you have seen how kind the Lord is to you. When we come back to conquer Jericho, gather all your family and tie a piece of red cord in the window so we know which house is yours. We will not lay a hand on anyone in your family. But if you tell anyone about us, we will not keep this promise."

Rahab agreed, tied the cord in her window, and sent the men on their way.

After three days of hiding in the hills, the spies returned to Joshua at Shittim, saying, "One thing is very clear: the Lord wants to give us this land. The people living there trembled with fear when they heard we were coming...except one, named Rahab."

Even though Rahab had sinned against God, her heart had turned towards Him in repentance. She was sorry for her sin, and wanted to follow God instead. So, instead of being treated like a Canaanite, Rahab would be treated as an Israelite.

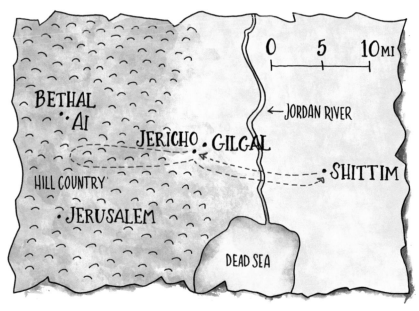

Still today, every one of us has sin in our lives. We deserve to be treated like Canaanites. After all, our sin deserves death! Instead, those who turn in faith to Jesus are welcomed into God's own family.

Throughout the Bible, the Canaanites are not without hope. Those like Rahab, who turn to God in faith, can enjoy life with Him.

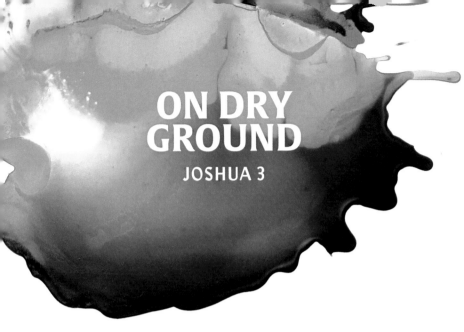

ON DRY GROUND

JOSHUA 3

Early the next morning, Joshua sensed the time had come to enter the Promised Land.

After three days spent camping at the edge of the river, the officers went through the camp, exclaiming, "The time has come to go over the river! When you see the priests carrying the ark of the covenant of the Lord, follow it. But do not go near the ark. In fact, stay one half-mile from it so everyone can see the ark as it leads us forward."

You may have heard about the ark of the covenant before, but perhaps you haven't. It was very important to the people of Israel. Picture a large box made of wood and decorated with beautiful, sculpted gold. It was the presence of God among the people, and so only the priests were allowed to carry it. No one else was to go anywhere near the ark.

The next day, Joshua gave the priests the long-awaited words. "Take the ark of the covenant and go before the people." In a sense, Joshua was saying, "Friends, it's time to go home."

As the priests carried the ark, the Lord spoke to Joshua, saying, "Today I will make you the leader of Israel so that the people will know that I am with you just as I was with Moses. Now, tell the priests that they are to stand still in the Jordan River with the ark of the covenant."

Now you should know that the Jordan is not a tiny, little creek. It's actually one of the most dangerous rivers on the planet. What could God mean?! On a normal day, the waters are 100 feet across and up to ten feet deep. But, this was not a normal day. Instead, because of the spring rains, the wild waters of the Jordan had overflowed its banks. The river was nearly one mile across and 100 feet deep!

Joshua encouraged the people, saying, "Come and hear the word of the Lord. Then you will know that He is with us. And if He is with us, the Canaanites don't stand a chance!

"Let the ark pass before you into the Jordan. Then, assign one man from each tribe of Israel (twelve in all) to follow the priests. When the priest's feet step into the waters of the Jordan River, the river will stop and the water will pile up in a big heap." Crazy, right!?

And then it happened, just as Joshua said.

The priests dipped their toes from the hot sand of Moab into the Jordan for the first time, and...

...God stopped the water. Amazingly, billions and billions of gallons of river water rose up in a gigantic heap eighteen miles away!

Then the priests carrying the ark of the covenant and all of Israel miraculously walked into the Promised Land on dry ground. After hundreds of years, they were home. But home, they would soon learn, looked much, much different now.

TWELVE STONES

JOSHUA 4

After forty long years with hot desert sand stuck between their toes, God's people were finally home. But before they left the Jordan, God wanted His people to remember.

The Lord told Joshua, "Choose twelve men, one from each tribe. Each man should take a stone from the middle of the Jordan to the place where you sleep tonight."

Joshua called the twelve men together, saying, "These stones will be a reminder to you. When your children ask, 'What are these dusty old rocks here for?', tell them about the time the Lord stopped the waters of the Jordan River as the ark of the covenant passed before you. These stones will help you remember the miracle that God did for you and for His glory."

The people did just as Joshua asked. The stones are there to this day. (See Kaleidoscope Corner for more on this.)

This is the first of seven moments in Joshua involving stones. We will make note of them as we go through this book. The stones helped the people of God remember, but today they help us see Jesus with even greater meaning and clarity.

In the book of Psalms, David writes that Jesus will be "the stone the builders rejected" but that this stone would "become the cornerstone." Without a cornerstone, buildings collapse.

The New Testament tells us that the family of God is like a building with Jesus as the cornerstone. The people of God don't have to worry, because they have the strongest foundation of all time!

The stones in Joshua remind us of what God has done and what He will do to save us from our greatest enemy - sin.

The priests continued to stand with the ark of the covenant in the middle of the Jordan until all of God's people crossed over and everything God had commanded of Joshua and Moses was done.

That day, more than 40,000 people passed over the Jordan and into the plains of Jericho. The Lord raised Joshua up as the leader of Israel. God's people stood in awe of him just as they stood in awe of Moses.

Then Joshua commanded the priests to come out of the Jordan. As soon as they passed over, the waters of the river surged back together, overflowing their banks just as before.

And Joshua, looking again at the twelve stones, explained once again to the people, "When your children ask in times to come, 'What are these dusty old rocks here for?' tell them that Israel passed over the Jordan on dry ground because the Lord dried up the waters just as He did to the Red Sea. God did this so that all the people of the earth would know that the hand of the Lord is mighty and so that you would honor and respect the Lord your God forever."

Remembering - it's a big theme in the Bible. Remembering is especially important in the book of Joshua. In the books on either side of Joshua, especially those of Exodus and Numbers and then again in Judges, there is a lot of forgetting. The people of God forget who made them, provides for them, and loves them.

But here in Joshua, at least for the moment, God's people remembered. God is gracious and compassionate, slow to anger, and abounding in unchanging, rock solid love.

Kaleidoscope Corner
Are The Stones *Really* Still There?

Hunter Creek winds through the middle of our neighborhood. In the summer, I like to take my kids (who are 8, 6, 4, and 1 at the printing of this book) down to the creek to play.

One day we got to wondering...if we built a pile of rocks in the middle of the creek, would it survive the next storm?

So, we carefully built an experimental tower of stones about two feet tall. But when we came to check on it after the next storm, the tower was gone!

If our pile of rocks couldn't survive a measly thunderstorm, how are we to believe a pile of rocks set up near the Jordan thousands of years ago is still there? (Perhaps I'm the only one who asks weird questions like this!)

To answer this curious question, we must remember that the Bible was not written to us. We get to enjoy it and it's our only authority for life even thousands of years after Joshua. But the first audience of the Bible was Israel. So, we can imagine that the stones may have been there "to *that* day" even if they are not there to *our* day.

A similar passage in 2 Chronicles 5 says that the poles used to carry the ark of the covenant are in Solomon's temple "to this day." But that temple and the ark have since been destroyed.

Both of these examples help us to remember that the Bible was written at a specific time in history to a specific group of people.

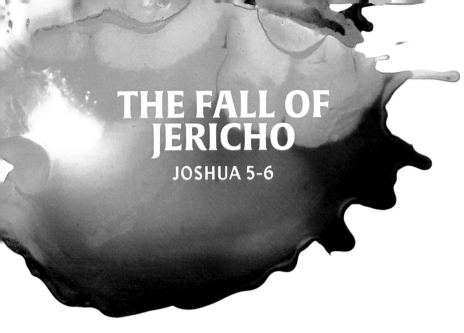

THE FALL OF JERICHO

JOSHUA 5-6

The Canaanites trembled with fear as Israel crossed over the Jordan. Deep down, they knew they were in big trouble!

But before Israel could go to battle, they had a few things on their to-do list.

Remember, Israel had wandered with hot desert sand stuck between their toes for 40 years as a punishment *and* to rid Israel of unfaithfulness. God was literally waiting for all the people who did not obey Him to die. He promised that those who had been unfaithful would never see the Promised Land - a lush and gorgeous land He said was flowing with milk and honey.

But even as the people of God wandered in the desert, they continued in their unfaithfulness. For example, God commanded Israel to put a mark, called circumcision, on the body of every boy when they were just eight days old. This mark showed that they belonged to God. But, during those years in the desert, the leaders did not do as they were told.

But now, out of his deep faithfulness to God, Joshua made knives and circumcised all the men and all the boys.

"Like a stone being rolled off your neck, today I have rolled away the punishment you deserve for your unfaithfulness," the Lord assured Joshua. And so, the place Israel camped was named Gilgal, which means "to roll."

It was as if God was turning the page for Israel, saying, "Today is a brand new day!"

For the time being, Israel was full of faith.

Sometime later, Joshua was near Jericho when a man appeared before him with a sword. Joshua asked, "Are you for us, or our enemies?"

"I am the commander of the Lord's army," the man said.

Joshua immediately fell to the ground, knowing the Lord was with him. "What are we to do now?" Joshua anxiously asked.

"Remove your sandals. The place you are standing is holy ground," the commander said. Joshua kicked off his sandals as quickly as he could.

One thing was clear: this land belonged to the Lord. And the battle they were about to fight was not just any battle. The battle belonged to the Lord and His people were only to listen and obey.

The Lord spoke to Joshua, saying, "I have given the city of Jericho to you. Here's your battle plan: all of your men will march around the city one time each day for six days. Seven priests will go with you with seven trumpets made of rams' horns while carrying the ark of the covenant. On the seventh day, everyone will march around the city seven times. Then, the priests will blow their trumpets and all the people will shout with loud voices. The strong walls of Jericho will fall flat and you will invade the city."

It was a strange plan, indeed. Marching, horn blowing, shouting!? And what about God saying that He had already given Jericho to Joshua before a sword was even drawn?*

Would Joshua believe God?

Joshua called all the priests and people together to explain God's plan. Immediately the priests, eager to destroy Jericho, hoisted the ark up on their shoulders and began to blow their trumpets. But, of course, nothing happened.

"No, no, no," Joshua explained, "you must wait for the right time." Joshua actually believed in God's bonkers-sounding plan!

So the soldiers and the priests with the ark and their trumpets marched around the city of Jericho for six days.

On the seventh day, they rose early, just as the sun was creeping over the horizon. Seven times the soldiers and the priests with the ark and their trumpets marched around the city.

On the seventh lap, the priests blew their trumpets as Joshua yelled, "Shout, for the Lord has given Jericho to you!"

Just then, Joshua remembered one special person...Rahab. "Whatever you do, don't lay a finger on Rahab and her family. Keep them safe. But everything else belongs to the Lord. Shatter it all and do not take anything for yourself."

The destruction of Jericho was not to be taken lightly. It was a serious matter. God knew that if the Israelites kept anything from the city, they may start to love the gods of the Canaanites more than Him.

And then it happened, just as God said. The horns blew, the people shouted, the walls fell flat, and Israel invaded and destroyed all of Jericho.

The soldiers burned the city with scorching flames of fire. Only the silver and gold, and vessels of bronze and iron were saved and put into the Lord's treasury.

But the two men who had spied out the land went to Rahab and saved her and all her family. Rahab's family lived with Israel for the rest of their lives.

Rahab, as it turned out, was quite an important addition for Israel! This woman, who was once an outcast forced to live as a sitting duck in the walls of her city, became the great-great-grandmother of King David - the most famous king in Israel's history. And do you know who was born into King David's family 28 generations later?

Jesus.

Jesus lived a perfect life, but He did not come from a perfect family. But that shows us all the more what God truly values in His kingdom.

In the book of Job, one of Job's friends proclaims that our God "sets the lowly in high places." Rahab is perhaps the greatest example of God treasuring those the world says are worthless. You might say that the kingdom of God is an "upside-down" kingdom where the weak become strong, the poor become rich, and the outsider become an insider!

God said this a number of times in Joshua to show that the battle was so certain, it was as if it was already over.

Kaleidoscope Corner
What's With All the Violence?

If you noticed a lot of violence in the last chapter, you are not alone! The book of Joshua brings up a lot of questions about how God could command His people to kill others. Doesn't God tell us to love our enemies?

If you're asking these questions, it shows that you understand a lot about God. You deserve a thoughtful answer!

First, we need to know that the Canaanites had grown very evil! They even sacrificed little children (see Deuteronomy 12:29-31). God did not want His people to be polluted by this evil as they moved back into their homeland.

Second, you'll see phrases in Joshua like "totally destroy" and "leave no survivors" which seem incredibly violent. But you should know that these phrases are what we call "hyperbole." Hyperbole (pronounced hyper-bow-lee) is a way of exaggerating to make a point (why do we *always* have lima beans at dinner!?).

In Deuteronomy 7, God commanded Israel not to marry or make business deals with the Canaanites when they live in the Promised Land again. But, if all the Canaanites were supposed to be dead, then why would this command exist? Also, God was very open to Canaanites who turned to Him throughout Joshua, like Rahab and the Gibeonites (you'll meet them later).

Finally, this was a unique command for a short period of time in history. This violence was limited to the Canaanites living in the Promised Land and in no way is a command to be used today. In all other situations, God asked his people to live in peace with their neighbors (see Deuteronomy 20).

THE GOOD TIMES END

JOSHUA 7

God's instructions seemed simple enough. March around the city, blow the trumpets, destroy the city, take nothing with you. But one man, named Achan, did not listen and the Lord's anger burned like fire on the people of Israel.

The next city to be conquered was called Ai. Just like before, Joshua first sent spies to scout out the city. But when the spies returned, their report was much different than at Jericho.

"The people of Ai are weak!" the spies boasted. "We don't even need an entire army. Only send 3,000 people. We will squash them like ants - no problem! "

Joshua listened to the spies and sent 3,000 soldiers. But when the soldiers saw the men of Ai, their hearts sank with fear. The Israelite soldiers fled as quickly as possible, but still, the men of Ai killed 36 Israelites that day. As it turned out, following the spies' smug advice instead of God was not just a bad idea. It was deadly!

Joshua was devastated. He tore his clothes in agony as he bowed in prayer before the ark of the covenant for hours upon hours.

"Why, God!?" Joshua pleaded, "Why have You brought us all this way only to destroy us? O Lord, we now look weak because You are against us. All the nations will wipe us from the face of the earth. What will You do?"

Then the Lord said to Joshua, "Get up! Your people, Israel, have sinned. They have forgotten My promises and My commands at Jericho. They have stolen and lied!"

Joshua was confused. Who lied?

The Lord continued, "Get up! Cleanse your people of this sin and destroy what you stole. Tell the people to get ready to meet with the Lord. Your enemies will defeat you until you rid yourselves of the things you stole.

"In the morning, bring all the tribes together. I will choose one clan from one tribe. Within that clan, I will choose one family. Each man in that family will come to Me, one by one. The man who stole will be burned with fire. He has forgotten My promises, broken My covenant, and done an outrageous, deadly thing in Israel!"

The next day it happened just as the Lord said. God chose the clan of the Zerahites, from the tribe of Judah. From the clan of the Zerahites, the family of Zabdi was taken.

When Zabdi's son Achan drew near, Joshua commanded, "Son, give glory to God. Do not hide what you have done."

Achan answered, "I have sinned against the Lord. When I was in Jericho, I saw a beautiful coat, five pounds of silver, and one pound of gold. I had to have them and now they are hidden in a hole under my tent."

Joshua sent messengers to check under the tent. It was just as Achan said.

The messengers brought the coat and the gold and the silver back to Joshua and he laid all the stolen goods before the Lord.

Then Joshua and all the people of Israel took Achan, the silver, the cloak, the gold, as well as his sons, daughters, oxen, donkeys, sheep, tent, and all he had to a valley.

And all the people of Israel threw stones and burned Achan and his family with fire until they all died and there was nothing left but a smoldering pile of ashes.

Achan, as it turns out, was the other side of the coin from Rahab. Though he was an Israelite, Achan was treated as a Canaanite. Though she was a Canaanite, Rahab was treated like an Israelite.

God has always, from the beginning to the end of the Bible, looked not at where you're from or what you look like. Instead, He knows your heart.

That day, a great heap of stones was raised over Achan along with all of his family and animals and belongings.

This pile of stones was quite unlike the pile of 12 stones from the Jordan. These rocks, rather than reminding Israel of God's faithfulness, told the story of His people's sin. To this day, the valley where Achan is buried is called the Valley of Achor, which means Valley of Trouble.

Once the stones were raised, the Lord's anger faded and He turned His face back toward Israel.

Sin, as we learn from Achan, is more serious than we'd like to think. It deserves death. Achan had to pay the awful price for his sin. Only then could God turn His face back toward Israel.

But, Jesus is the stone that does not crush His friends. Instead, He gives life to those who hate their sin and have faith in Him. Jesus took the punishment for all of our sins. Only because of Jesus's death can God look at us and promise that He will never leave us or forget us.

TURNING BACK

JOSHUA 8

Now that Achan was gone, there was still the little problem of Ai. What would Joshua do about this city that so easily defeated Israel?

"Take all your soldiers and go back to Ai," the Lord said to Joshua. "You will surely defeat them as you did Jericho. Only, please, this time, do not steal and hide things!"

Joshua knew the Lord was serious and so he took 30,000 men with him (ten times as many as before!). As he stood before his soldiers, Joshua delivered the battle plan. "Just as you did before, when the men from Ai come out, run away and make them chase you. But some of you, hide close to the city. When all their soldiers have left, go in and take the city. Burn everything you find. The Lord your God has given it to you!"

So, Joshua sent 5,000 men to hide west of the city. The other 25,000 men went with Joshua north of the city and camped there.

In the morning, the king of Ai saw the army of 25,000 and sent his men to battle. But Joshua and all Israel pretended to be defeated and fled toward the wilderness, just as the Lord commanded.

After some time, Ai was completely emptied as they chased the 25,000 Israelites into the wilderness. Ai thought they'd won, but instead, Israel had them right where they wanted.

As the people of Ai abandoned their city, the Lord said to Joshua, "Stretch out your javelin toward Ai!"

Joshua's javelin, as it turned out, was the sign for the hidden soldiers to move into the city. Israel, with nothing in the way, quickly captured the city and set it ablaze.

The people of Ai looked back over their shoulders to the terrifying sight of smoke billowing up from their beloved city. There was nowhere for the soldiers of Ai to go when the 25,000 fleeing Israelites turned around against them.

Once the city was nothing but a smoldering pile of ashes and everything in it was destroyed, Joshua finally lowered his javelin to signal that the battle was over. The mighty soldiers of Israel struck down every man in Ai. There were none left. Nobody survived...except one.

The king of Ai was spared and brought to Joshua.

At sunset, Joshua personally killed the king of Ai, buried him at the gate of the city, and raised up a heap of stones over his body. Those stones are there to this day.

Twelve stones from the Jordan to remember God's faithfulness.

Stones over Achan to mourn Israel's sin.

The king of Ai, buried under stones. A sign that God's favor had returned to the people of God.

Then Joshua built an altar of uncut stones to the Lord. He made it just as the Lord commanded. It would be a place of worship for Joshua and God's people.

At the altar, in the presence of the Lord and all the people, Joshua carved a copy of the law of Moses (another name for the Bible at the time) in stone. This was the fourth stone monument in Joshua: stones to know the love of God.

All Israel gathered together between Mount Gerizim and Mount Ebal, just as Moses had commanded (see Deuteronomy 27). The priests, before the ark of the covenant, blessed the people of Israel.

Then Joshua read the words of the law, both the blessings and the curses.

There was not a word of all that Moses commanded that Joshua did not read to Israel that day.

The Lord had turned back to Israel.

Israel had turned back to the Lord.

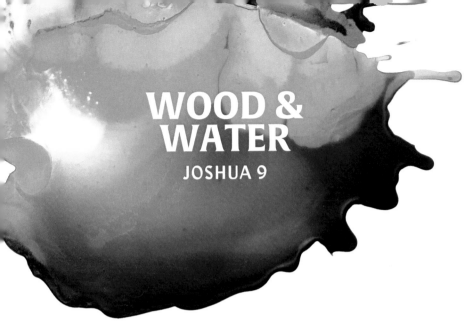

WOOD & WATER

JOSHUA 9

One by one, the kings of other Canaanite cities heard what happened at Jericho and Ai. Together, they wondered nervously, "Are we next?"

Several kings joined together to fight Israel, knowing they would be much stronger together than apart.

But one city decided to go it alone - Gibeon.

When the residents of Gibeon heard what Joshua did to Jericho and Ai, they devised a clever trick that involved fastening worn-out saddles on their donkeys and dressing in torn and tattered clothes.

The Gibeonites went to Joshua at Gilgal, pleading, "We have come from a faraway country and do not know where we are or what dangers lie ahead. Will you make a covenant, a promise, to protect us?"

This, of course, was a lie. The Gibeonites had only traveled five measly miles from home.

"Who are you? Where do you come from?" Joshua asked.

"We want to be your servants," the Gibeonites explained. "Our elders heard that the Lord is with you and that He has given you great success against your enemies."

What would Joshua do? These men seemed nice enough and they certainly appeared to need a home and protection.

But Joshua didn't know that the Gibeonites were actually his enemies!

So Joshua foolishly made peace with the Gibeonites and agreed to let them live with the Israelites. But, just a short time later, Israel learned the truth.

The next time Israel set out for battle, they traveled to four different cities. One of them was - you guessed it - Gibeon!

Israel could not do what God had asked of them. They could not destroy Gibeon because of the unwise agreement. Israel had disobeyed God once again.

Joshua called to the Gibeonites, saying, "Why did you fool us? Now you are cursed. You will be our servants."

"We lied because we know the Lord is with you. If you came to our city, surely we would have been destroyed. So, whatever seems good and right, you should do to us."

Joshua did not destroy Gibeon. Instead, he made them cutters of wood and gatherers of water - the worst of all the jobs of all the servants.

This story of the Gibeonites is a peculiar one. On the one hand, Israel disobeyed.

In the book of Deuteronomy, which they had just read in the previous chapter (remember Joshua writing and reading all of Moses's words?), Israel was told not to make any agreements like this with other nations. (See Kaleidoscope Corner for more on this.)

However, the Gibeonites remind us of another Canaanite who believed in God and was spared - Rahab.

So what's the point?

Did the Israelites disobey? Yes.

Did the Gibeonites trust God? It appears so.

So did God use Israel's disobedience for good? Perhaps He did!

The Bible often makes us wonder about God. It sets up confusing questions like these.

We can hold onto these puzzling issues by remembering that God is God and we are merely His people. We don't and can't understand all His ways, but we do know that He has promised to work all things together for the good of those who love Him. One day, when we see Him face to face, we will be able to ask Him all that has made us curious.

Kaleidoscope Corner
Why Not Be Neighborly?

Why was it so bad for Israel to be nice to the Gibeonites? After all, it seemed like they had come to trust in the Lord.

For our answer, we have to go back to the book of Deuteronomy. In Deuteronomy 20:17, we read that Israel must completely destroy the Hivites. The Gibeonites were a part of the Hivites.

Strike one.

Secondly, the leaders of Israel do not talk to the Lord about this decision. In Deuteronomy 10 (and many other places), Israel is commanded to follow God with all their heart and soul. This, of course, would include asking the Lord for advice, especially with big decisions like this.

Strike two.

Finally, Israel was commanded not to make any covenants with other nations in Deuteronomy 7. A covenant is a promise that cannot be broken and Israel was not to tie themselves to other nations in this way. While Israel was to make peace with nations outside of the Canaanites, in no way were they to enter into covenants with other nations!

Strike three.

For all of these reasons, the foolish agreement with the Gibeonites was a big strikeout for Israel!

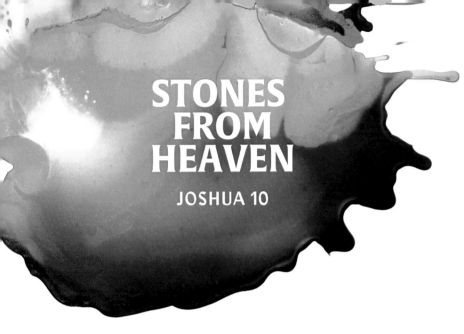

STONES FROM HEAVEN

JOSHUA 10

Just a short time later, a man named Adoni-zedek, the Canaanite king of Jerusalem, heard about Israel's stunning victories over Ai and Jericho as well as the peaceful (and unwise) arrangement they had with the Gibeonites.

Adoni-zedek grew fearful. With Gibeon on their side, Israel would certainly be unstoppable!

So Adoni-zedek sent messages to other Canaanite kings: Hoham of Hebron, Piram of Jarmuth, Japhia of Lachish, and Debir of Eglon, saying, "Come with me. Let's defeat Gibeon together!"

They all agreed and together went to make war against Gibeon.

But the men of Gibeon heard about the Canaanites' plan before they could attack and quickly sent word to Joshua, "Come now! The Canaanites are out to get us!"

Joshua left Gilgal right away and took every soldier with him. The Lord said to Joshua, "Do not fear, for I have given all these Canaanites into your hands. Not a man will remain standing when you're finished."

Joshua and his men marched all through the night, uphill, over a distance of fifteen miles. That sounds exhausting!

As Israel arrived, the Lord threw the Canaanites into a panic, driving them 30 miles away and clearing the way for Israel's victory. But this battle was far from over. The Lord had something else in mind!

Suddenly, large hailstones hurled down from heaven, striking Canannite after Canaanite. More men died that day from the hailstones than were killed with swords!

As for the fate of the Canaanite kings, their fear of Israel showed what spineless leaders they really were. While their soldiers were being struck down by swords and hailstones, they hid like cowards in a cave. Some help they were!

Joshua, using their weakness against them, told his soldiers to cover the cave with stones as Israel defeated the Canaanites.

This, curiously enough, is the fifth stone monument in Joshua. A gracious reminder of God's protection, even after the unwise promise made to the Gibeonites.

Joshua spoke to the Lord in the sight of all Israel, "Sun, stand still. Moon, stand still." And in one outstanding cosmic miracle, God made the sun and moon stop in their places until Israel finished defeating their enemies. (See Kaleidoscope Corner for more on this.)

The God who made the universe and all that is in it was clearly on the side of Israel, giving them all the time they needed to win the battle.

When Israel had defeated all their enemies so that there was not a single soldier who even moved his tongue against the people of Israel, the cowardly kings of the Amorites were allowed out of the cave.

Joshua killed the gutless kings and hung them in trees until evening - just as he did at Ai.

But Joshua was not done yet. From there, Israel traveled south. One by one, they captured each of the Canaanite kings' cities; Libnah, Lachish, Gezer, Eglon, Hebron, and Debir were all defeated. Not a single person was left standing. Everything was destroyed, just as the Lord commanded.

Joshua defeated all these kings and captured their land at one time because God fought for Israel.

Then Joshua, and all of Israel with him, returned to Gilgal.

Kaleidoscope Corner
Did the Sun Really Stand Still?

If you've been keeping score in Joshua, you've seen the Lord do a lot of miracles. The parting of the Jordan and the walls of Jericho falling flat are two of the most memorable.

But, for some reason, the sun standing still in Joshua 10 trips a lot of people up! Perhaps it seems a bit too much like a fairy tale to be believable.

The first thing to say is that when we believe the Bible, we have to believe all of it. To choose to believe that God could perform one miracle but not another is to say that we get to decide what did and didn't happen instead of God. To do that is to put ourselves in place of God, and that does not usually end up being a very good idea!

Second, this is not the only time this happens in the Bible. In 2 Kings 20:9-11, the sun's shadow doesn't just stand still. Instead, it moves backward!

Third, it seems that the writer of Joshua almost counts on the readers going, "Huh!? Did that really happen?" In a small detail, the writer includes what's called a secondary source - the Book of Jashar. While the Book of Jashar is not in the Bible, it was clearly written around the same time as Joshua and makes mention of this miracle as well. If two witnesses record the same event, it shows that it's more likely to have actually happened.

Finally, we should not doubt that the God who made the sun, also has control over it. He instantly calms storm-tossed seas, makes bushes burn without being consumed, and can certainly make the sun stand still!

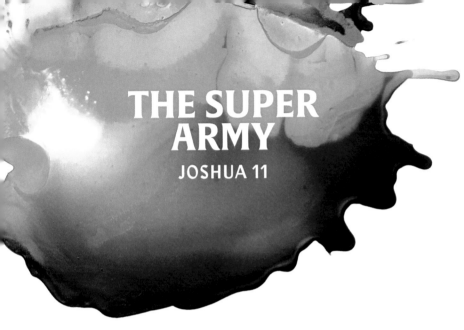

THE SUPER ARMY

JOSHUA 11

As soon as Israel crossed the Jordan, life for the Canaanites changed forever. For many, many years they had been able to do, more or less, whatever they wanted in the Promised Land. But now, Israel was back...and God was with them.

The Lord was undeniably in control, giving Israel victory after victory, even after their mistake with the Gibeonites!

Jabin, the Canaanite king of Hazor, caught wind of Israel's conquests and knew he would soon be in the crosshairs. So, he joined forces with other Canaanite kings in Madon, Shimron, and Achshaph (if you are having a hard time pronouncing all these words...don't worry, so does everyone else!).

Jabin also called on a host of other kings in the northern hill country, and in the Arabah south of the Sea of Galilee, and in the lowland, and Naphoth-dor to the west, to the Canaanites in the east and west, the Amorites, the Hittites, the Perizzites, and the Jebusites in the hill country, and the Hivites under Hermon in the land of Mizpah. Whew! That was a long list...and a lot of people who would like nothing better than to squash Israel!

To carry out their Israelite-squashing plan, the kings agreed to form a massive super-army. Counting the soldiers, chariots, and horses lined up against Israel would have been like counting sand on a seashore - impossible!

The Israelite-squashing super-army, with their glittering chariots and horses, gathered at the waters of Merom ready to crush anyone and anything.

Can you imagine what Joshua must have felt at that moment? Heart racing, sweaty palms...what would happen?!

God must have known and so He comforted Joshua, saying, "Do not be afraid. By tomorrow, at this time, I will give all of these people into your hands. You will cut the hamstrings of all their horses so they are useless in battle. You will burn all their chariots with fire."

How could God make such a gutsy prediction? How would this only take 24 hours? Didn't He know this was the largest army Israel had ever faced?

But, just as before, the Lord was right! Joshua and his soldiers traveled north from Gilgal to fight and the Lord triumphed over all of Israel's enemies.

In fact, all those mighty armies didn't stand a chance! Instead, they ran away with their tails between their legs to the coast near Sidon and into the Valley of Mizpah. But Joshua's men chased them down and destroyed them all. The Israelites cut the hamstrings of the horses and burned all their chariots, just as the Lord said. Every enemy soldier was killed, even Jabin, the king of Hazor.

Israel burned Hazor with fire, as they had done to Jericho and Ai. Joshua captured all the cities and destroyed the people. Israel took their belongings, all the riches, and livestock, just as the Lord commanded.

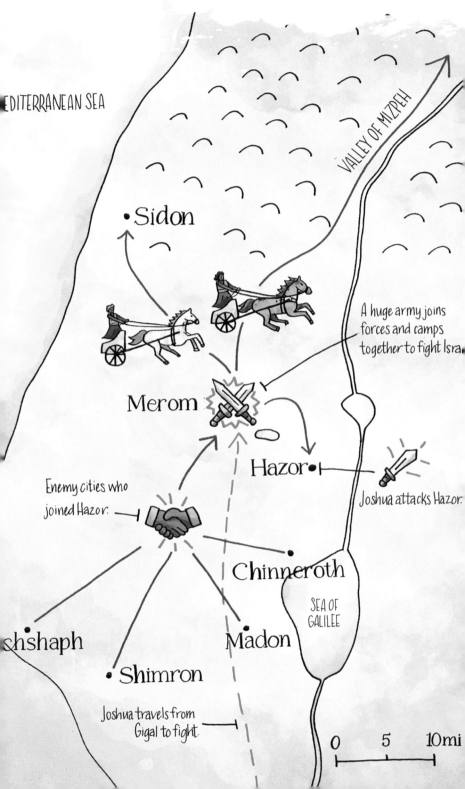

MEDITERRANEAN SEA

Sidon

VALLEY OF MIZPEH

Merom

A huge army joins forces and camps together to fight Isra.

Hazor

Joshua attacks Hazor.

Enemy cities who joined Hazor.

Chinneroth

SEA OF GALILEE

chshaph

Madon

Shimron

Joshua travels from Gigal to fight.

0   5   10mi

In all of Joshua's battles, he made peace with only one city - Gibeon. In every other case, Joshua did all that Moses and the Lord asked of him.

Then Joshua gave each tribe of Israel a gift - land. This gift had been promised long ago to their great-great-great (and many more greats) grandfather, Abraham.

Now, finally, the land had rest from war and Israel was home.

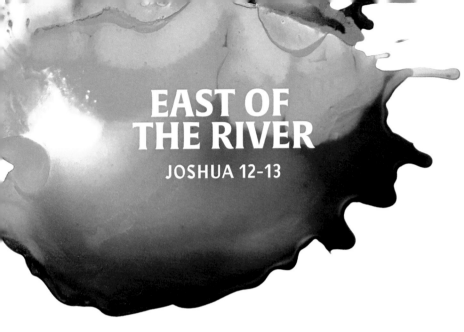

EAST OF
THE RIVER
JOSHUA 12-13

The end of Chapter 11 wraps up the battles and conquests of Joshua. Most of the next part of the book tells of how the Promised Land was divided among the 12 tribes of Israel.

Let's be honest for a minute - this section of the book can seem quite uninteresting, especially when compared with the first half of the book! But remember this as you read: all of this really did happen and it really did matter!

Real men and women traveled hundreds of miles with hot desert sand between their toes. Actual battles were fought and real people died.

Plus, this was the exact land that was promised to Abraham all those many, many years ago. The Lord told Abraham that he would have children as numerous as the stars in the sky, even though he was an old man. Those children, He said, would live in a special land...the Promised Land. Now what once seemed like a distant dream was happening right before their eyes.

First, let's back up a moment before going forward.

Before Joshua became the leader of Israel, before Israel crossed the Jordan, and before Jericho, Ai, and Hazor were defeated, Moses did some conquering of his own.

On the east side of the Jordan, Moses defeated Sihon, king of the Amorites. Sihon lived at Heshbon and ruled the land from Aroer, on the edge of the Valley of the Arnon, and from the middle of the valley as far as the river Jabbok, which is the boundary of the Ammonites.

Moses also defeated Og, the king of Bashan, who ruled over Mount Hermon and Salecah and all Bashan to the boundary of the Geshurites and Maacathites, and over half of Gilead to the boundary with Sihon king of Heshbon.

The land Moses conquered belonged to the tribes of Reuben, Gad, and the half-tribe of Manasseh.

On the other side of the Jordan, Joshua defeated a tremendous number of Canaanite kings. We have heard of most of these before, but they are worth listing here, just to stand amazed at the sheer number of victories: Jericho, Ai, Jerusalem, Hebron, Jarmuth, Lachish, Eglon, Gezer, Debir, Geder, Hormah, Arad, Libnah, Adullam, Makkedah, Bethel, Tappuah, Hepher, Aphek, Lasharon, Madon, Hazor, Shimron-meron, Achshaph, Taanach, Megiddo, Kedesh, Jokneam, Dor, Goiim, and Tizrah!

Congratulations if you made it through that entire list! That was 31 victories in all!

Now, after all these overpowering wins, Joshua was not the young man he used to be! The Lord said to him, "You are old, and you have clearly won many lands! And yet there is still much more land to conquer.

"This is the land that remains: all the land of the Philistines, the Geshurites, and the Avvim. The Philistines have five rulers: in Gaza, Ashdod, Ashkelon, Gath, and Ekron. This land stretches from the Shihor, which is east of Egypt, northward to the boundary with Ekron.

"There also remains the Canaanite land to the south, and Mearah that belongs to the Sidonians, to Aphek, to the boundary of the Amorites, and the land of the Gebalites, and all of Lebanon towards the east, from Baal-gad below Mount Hermon to Lebo-hamath."

That sure sounded like a lot of work to Joshua - far too much for a man in his later years! But Joshua never was and never would be alone.

The Lord continued, "Do not fear. I will do the conquering for you, Joshua. My only command is to divide the land among the tribes as an inheritance. This was My promise, and I intend to keep it."

The tribe of Levi was the only tribe that did not receive any land, only cities to live in. The Levites served as assistants to the priests and their inheritance was said to be in the offerings they made to God.

The Lord then gave very detailed instructions on how to divide the land among the tribes. If you read about it in your Bible, it may seem quite long! But, remember and listen. The land, as we already said, was important and many of the boundaries were reminders of places the Lord did amazing things for the people of God.

Reuben's land was from Aroer, which is on the edge of the Valley of Arnon. Included was the land where Balaam was killed by the sword by the people of Israel (you can read about that in Numbers 22-24). Reuben also had a border with the Jordan River.

Gad's land was Jazer, all the cities of Gilead, and half the land of the Ammonites, to Aroer. Included in Gad's land was the city of Succoth, where Jacob built a house in the book of Genesis.

Gad also received the land once controlled by King Sihon of the Amorites (see Numbers 21:23-24). Gad shared a boundary to the west with the Jordan and their land extended south to the Sea of Galilee.

The tribe of Manasseh was divided into two smaller half-tribes. Half of the tribe of Manasseh received land east of the Jordan. Their region extended from Mahanaim and through all of Bashan. Most notably, it included the former kingdom of Og (see Numbers 21:31-35) and all the towns of Jair (which becomes important in Judges 10).

WEST OF THE RIVER

JOSHUA 14-15

If you thought dividing the land to the west of the Jordan River would be a piece of cake, well, you'd be wrong! At nearly 8,000 square miles (the size of the state of New Hampshire) this was no small task!

The people of God did everything the Lord commanded Moses. The land was to be divided by casting lots. This was sort of like drawing names out of a hat. It made the distribution of land fair and protected the leaders from showing favoritism.

But before they started, the people of the tribe of Judah came to Joshua at Gilgal. Caleb stepped out from among the tribe and spoke to Joshua, saying, "When I was 40 years old, Moses sent me to spy out the land. He promised that the land I found would be mine to give to my children. I'm now 85 years old and I'm as strong today as I was then. Give me the hill country of Hebron. I know the Anakim live there now with great cities, but the Lord will be with me and I will drive them out."

Now, you should know that the Anakim were famously humongous, powerful warriors. In Numbers, Moses said they made Israelites look like grasshoppers. Caleb was old, but he knew the Lord was with him, and no giant would stand in his way.

Joshua honored Moses's promise that day and gave Caleb the land of Hebron because he followed the Lord with his whole heart.

The people of Judah also received land that stretched south to the boundary with Edom to the wilderness of Zin. Their east boundary was the Salt Sea at the mouth of the Jordan River. Notably, within their bounds was the important city of Jerusalem. The west boundary was with the Mediterranean Sea as its coastline.

The tribe of Judah was given much land and many cities, and Caleb did defeat the gigantic Anakim living in the hill country of Hebron. But there remained a constant reminder of Judah's incomplete obedience: the Jebusites.

The Jebusites lived in the city of Jerusalem when the land was divided. Moses and Joshua were told time and time again to destroy all the people they found living in their land. God knew if they did not that their hearts would fall in love with the Canaanite gods.

Were the gods of the Jebusites more powerful than the one true God? Certainly not! Were the Jebusites more powerful than the mighty Anakim? Of course not!

But the people of God, for some reason, allowed the Jebusites to continue living in Jerusalem. It would forever be a reminder that sin makes our hearts turn from God to follow our own ways.

MANASSEH & EPHRAIM

JOSHUA 16-17

The family of Joseph (from the book of Genesis) was split into two tribes - Manasseh and Ephraim. Their land went from the Jordan River by Jericho into the hill country to Bethel. To the west, their land stretched to the Mediterranean Sea.

The tribe of Ephraim had an eastern boundary of Ataroth-addar. To the north was Michmethath. To the west was the Mediterranean Sea. Ephraim had the cities of Shiloh and Shechem, which is where Joseph was buried, as well as Mount Gerizim and Mount Ebal, where Joshua read the covenant to Israel in Joshua 8.

But just like the tribe of Judah, the Ephraimites did not drive out all the other nations living in their land. In their sin, they allowed the Canaanites living in Gezer to remain. This was a sad reminder of their unfaithfulness to God.

The people of Manasseh were divided into clans based on the families of the sons of Manasseh, who was a son of Joseph. One of the sons, Zelophehad, had only daughters. This was a big problem because only men were landowners in those days.

So, the daughters of Zelophehad went to Eleazar the priest and Joshua, saying, "The Lord told Moses to give us an inheritance of land along with our brothers."

Because of the Lord's kindness, Joshua gave the daughters the land Moses promised. This is a small detail in the book of Joshua, but it tells us a lot about God. He treasures all people - men and women. He did what no other king would do to care for His people.

The rest of the land for Manasseh was very large. On the north side was Asher. The land went all the way down to Michmethath (try to say that ten times fast!), which is just to the east of Shechem.

A small, marshy body of water called the Brook Kanah (which means brook of reeds) served as a boundary between Manasseh and Ephraim. Manasseh also shared a border with the tribe of Issachar.

Manasseh's land had many little towns and villages such as Dor and Megiddo. But the people of Manasseh could not defeat the Canaanites in these cities. Instead, they made them into servants. As you may remember from earlier chapters, this served as a continual reminder that Israel did not obey God completely.

Even though they were given much land, the tribes of Joseph were not happy because the land was full of steep mountains that were not very good for farming and building homes. The leaders spoke to Joshua, saying, "We have many people in our tribes, but you have not given us very much land."

Joshua instructed, "If you don't have enough land, you can go into the land of the Perizzites and the Rephaim to the south and west. This is forest land that we have yet to conquer."

"But the Canaanites live there!" the people retorted. "They are mighty warriors with chariots of iron! We could never defeat them."

Joshua looked at the people with strength and courage, reminding them, "Though they are strong and have chariots, you have the Lord."

Why did the people of Ephraim need this reminder?! After all, they had seen God's mighty hand at work before. The Canaanites feared Israel and would have likely fled even at the sight of an army sent by God!

But this was not the first or last time God's people needed this reminder. As you read further in the Bible you will see these doubts were just the beginning of Israel slipping away from God.

LOTS & LOTS OF LAND

JOSHUA 18-19

Then the whole congregation of the people of Israel gathered together at Shiloh. There, they set up the tent of meeting - also known as the tabernacle (you can read about this in Exodus 27:21 and 40:2).

What a glorious moment for Israel! One of the first things God told them to do once they settled in the Promised Land was to build a sanctuary, a place they could worship. God was with His people and they knew it.

As they met together, seven tribes had not received their land. So, Joshua instructed the seven remaining tribes to send out three men each to journey through the remaining land. They were to bring a report back to Joshua with descriptions of the land: Where are the rivers? Where are the hills? Where are the cities? Stuff like that.

Once Joshua had the report, he would divide the land seven ways. Joshua would then cast lots (just as before) to decide which tribe received each of the seven portions.

So, 21 Israelite men set out to survey the land. When they returned, an entire book of fieldnotes from the journey awaited Joshua.

Once again, Joshua began to cast lots and hand out the plots of land.

Benjamin received land between Judah and the people of Joseph (Ephraim and Manasseh). It was a small piece of land, but it included the city of Jericho, which was the very first city Joshua conquered. Benjamin's border on the east was with the Jordan River and they had a tiny strip of land that connected with the tribe of Reuben.

The second lot went to Simeon. Their land was an odd shape, indeed: a circle, carved out of the middle of the land belonging to Judah. As it turned out, the land Judah inherited was much too large for them (after they complained about not having enough!), so Simeon was a welcome addition for added protection!

The third lot went to the people of Zebulun. Theirs was a very small piece of land nestled right above and sharing a small sliver of a border with Manasseh.

The fourth lot was right next door to Zebulun and had a southern border with Manasseh. The land went to Issachar. While not large, the land included sixteen cities and had the Jordan River as its eastern border.

A fifth lot went to the tribe of Asher. Their land was a narrow strip that went up the coast of the Mediterranean Sea and shared a southern border with - you guessed it - Manasseh. Notably, the land given to Asher included the land that belonged to Sidon. Remember, back in Joshua 11, the super-army ran away with their tails between their legs, but the Israelites caught the runaways in Sidon and destroyed them.

Naphtali received the sixth parcel of land. Located in the northern part of the Promised Land, it shared an eastern border with the Jordan and the Sea of Galilee. To the south was the land given to Zebulun and Issachar and to the west was the land for Asher.

The final piece of land went to the tribe of Dan. But, as we learn later, in Judges 1:34, the Amorites took their land from them. After fleeing to the hill country near Mount Hermon, the tribe came down and captured the city of Leshem, which they renamed Dan.

Finally, the people of Israel gave an inheritance of land to Joshua. The Lord commanded that Joshua should receive any city he asked for.

But, rather than a big, important city, Joshua chose a small one in southwest Ephraim. The fact that Joshua waited until every tribe received their land is a hint of Joshua's growth into a true servant leader. In a sense, he laid down his life for others.

Joshua points the way to the one who was a greater and better Joshua - the leader Israel really longed for - Jesus.

Joshua cast lots for lots and lots of land. This land was God's promise, given to Abraham, and passed down to his children. But remember, God also promised to keep His covenant. God would protect His people.

He protected Israel from the Canaanites, but they were not actually Israel's biggest enemy - sin was. Israel deserved death, not from the Canaanites, but for their sin.

But God, being true to His covenant, sent His only son, Jesus, to die the death we deserve on the cross.

If you read very carefully, you'll notice something curious happened to Jesus. It reminds us of Joshua.

Jesus was stripped of His clothes on the way to the cross. His captors divided the clothing as weird souvenirs of sorts. How did they decide who got what piece of clothing?

They cast lots.

Lots cast for Israel, for God had kept His promise of land.

Lots cast for Jesus's clothing, for God had kept His promise of life for all who trust in Him.

THE LEVITES
JOSHUA 20-21

Throughout the Bible, the Lord shows His people more love than they deserve. This is called grace and God wanted to soak this newly divided land in a giant pool of His love.

So, God chose three cities on either side of the Jordan River to be cities of refuge: places where those who accidentally killed someone, or killed someone in an act of self-protection, could go for safety. Once in these cities, people were given a place to live until they could have a fair trial. (You can read more about cities of refuge in Numbers 35.)

So, they made Kedesh, Shechem, and Hebron the cities of refuge west of the Jordan and Bezer, Ramoth, and Golan the cities of refuge east of the Jordan.

God even went one step further. These cities not only offered protection for Israelites but were also open to people of other nations and those who were simply traveling through the land. Even in Joshua, there are whispers (and sometimes shouts) of God's love and kindness for the whole world.

But God was not done taking care of His people quite yet.

The leaders of the Levites came to Eleazar the priest and Joshua and to the heads of the families and tribes, saying, "The Lord commanded Moses to give us cities to live in and pastures to raise our animals and crops."

Without question, the people of Israel gave the Levites 48 cities to live in throughout the Promised Land, along with pastureland to raise animals and grow crops for food.

The tribe of Levi was divided into three families, depending on who your great-great-great-grandparents were. One family, the Kohathites, were given cities in the center and south of the Promised Land. The Gershonites and Merarites, the other two families, received land in the north and east.

Finally, all of Israel settled in the land and had peace all around them from war. Not one word of all the good promises that the Lord had made to the people of Israel, from Abraham to Joshua, had failed. All of them came true.

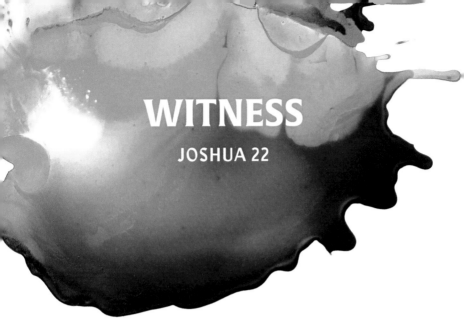

WITNESS

JOSHUA 22

Joshua gathered all the leaders of the tribes of Reuben, Gad, and half of the tribe of Manasseh to meet him at Shiloh. These, as you know by now, were the three tribes whose land was east of the Jordan.

Joshua encouraged the men, saying, "You have kept all of the commands of the Lord and have obeyed His voice. Now, the Lord has given us a time of peace. You are free to go back across the Jordan to the land God gave you. Love the Lord your God with all your heart and soul."

Joshua blessed the tribes, giving them livestock, silver, gold, bronze, iron, and clothing.

And so, the tribes of Reuben, Gad, and half of the tribe of Manasseh began their journey home.

When the tribes came to the western shore of the Jordan River, they built a stone altar (a place of worship). The altar was so large, it could be seen from both sides of the Jordan.

The other tribes soon heard about the altar and grew very concerned, for there was supposed to be only one altar to the Lord at Shiloh. Had Reuben, Gad, and half the tribe of Manasseh built an altar to another god?

Confused, the people of Israel gathered at Shiloh to make war against their fellow tribes. A civil war!? Who saw that coming?

But before launching an attack, the other nine-and-a-half tribes sent Phinehas, the son of Eleazar the priest as well as one chief from each tribe to reason with the eastern tribes.

Israel remembered the sin of Achan (look back at Chapter 7 if you've forgotten). If you recall, it was not just Achan who suffered for his sin, but the whole community of Israel. The people of God knew that sin is serious and always has disastrous consequences.

Phinehas and the chiefs arrived at the altar, asking, "What is this you have done?! Are you turning away from the Lord? Do you not remember the other times we turned from God? This never ever ends well for us!"

The people of Reuben, Gad, and half the tribe of Manasseh were shocked. They never meant to disobey the Lord!

In fact, they hadn't disobeyed at all.

The leaders of the eastern tribes answered, "The Mighty One, God, the Lord! The Mighty One, God, the Lord! He knows! If it was in sin that we built this, then you should not spare us today!

"But, no! We built this altar to make sure that our children would remember the Lord, the God of Israel. We did not build it for burnt offerings or sacrifice. We built it as a witness to the greatness of our God!"

When Phinehas the priest and the chiefs heard these words, joy welled up in their hearts. "Today we know that the Lord is with you," Phinehas celebrated.

Phinehas and the chiefs quickly returned home to tell their friends and families the good news. And the people of Israel praised the Lord and didn't speak anymore of war against the other tribes.

The eastern tribes called the stone altar "Witness." "For," they said, "it is a witness between us that the Lord is our God."

This was the sixth monument of stones in Joshua. Stones for future generations to know the love of God.

Kaleidoscope Corner
What's the Big Deal About a Second Altar?

Especially in my town of Tuscaloosa, Alabama, there seems to be a church on every corner. In fact, by God's good work, there are hundreds of thousands of Bible-believing churches all over the world. Perhaps you are a part of one!

So why was a second place of worship such a big deal in Joshua? The first thing to say is that altars in the Old Testament were very different from churches today. Altars were places of animal sacrifice and many other types of offerings. This, of course, is quite dissimilar from the churches we know and love today because Jesus is our once and for all sacrifice.

Secondly, God commanded that there be only one place of worship in Deuteronomy 12. Israel was not to set up for worship just anywhere, but rather in the one place that God would show them.

God commanded this because maintaining one altar helped Israel to remain pure in their worship. If they spread out to several different places it was likely their worship would have taken on the form of the Canaanites with less and less supervision.

Later in the Bible's story, God's people do set up a second altar in Dan. You can read about it in 1 Kings 12. Let's just say (spoiler alert!) it did not go well.

FAREWELL

JOSHUA 23-24

Many years passed for Israel, and Joshua grew very old. He summoned all of Israel. The elders and heads of the families and all of the judges and officers gathered around Joshua as he began to speak.

"As you can now see, I am old and frail," Joshua began. "You know and have seen all the Lord has done. He defeated all the nations that once lived in this land for you."

Then Joshua remembered that, although much land had been conquered, there were still miles and miles of land crawling with Canaanites, which rightfully belonged to the people of Israel. The conquest was still incomplete.

"The Lord your God will drive out the nations that still remain and you will live in the land fully, just as the Lord your God promised you. Because God is with you, even if there are 1,000 enemies and only one of you...they stand no chance. God will win!" Joshua encouraged them.

"Be strong and obey everything written in the Book of the Law of Moses (in other words, what they had of the Bible at the time). Cling to the Lord your God and do not follow the gods of the other nations. Love the Lord with all your heart and soul," Joshua urged the people.

Joshua knew his days were growing short. These may be his last words to his friends. "And now I am about to leave this earth and you will bury my body in the ground. But before I go, I want you to remember that the Lord has made all of His promises come true. He has failed at nothing. But, if you forget what He has commanded and what He has promised, your end will come quickly. If you serve other gods, the Lord's anger will burn against you."

At once Joshua gathered all the tribes of Israel to Shechem. To this point, he had only spoken to the leaders. Now, he was ready to talk to everyone.

To a sea of thousands upon thousands of people, Joshua began, "The Lord God says to you: 'Remember long ago when your fathers lived in another land? They served false gods. Then, I called Abraham and led him into Canaan, which is exactly where you now stand (see Genesis 12:6). I gave him a son in his old age, and he named him Isaac. To Isaac, I gave Jacob, who became Israel, and Esau. Esau and his family stayed in the hill country of Seir, on the very edge of the Promised Land. But Israel went down to Egypt.

"'But I did not leave Israel alone. No, I sent Moses and Aaron, and I sent plagues on Egypt. I rescued you, my beloved people, and brought you out.

"'Then your fathers came to the Red Sea as the Egyptians chased them on chariots and horseback. I saw this and parted the Red Sea to let you across. But then I slammed the waters shut on the Egyptians and destroyed them.

"'Your fathers then came to the land of the Amorites and the Moabites. I defeated them and gave you their land.

"'And then, remember, you crossed over the Jordan River. I gave you Jericho, and all the nations living there. These nations were terrified because I was with you.

"'I gave you land that you did not work for. You now live in cities that you did not build. You eat fruit and olives that you did not plant. I gave you all of this because I am a kind and generous God. I love you and I want you to know that deep inside your heart.'"

Then Joshua said these words, which would come to mean more than Israel could have known at the time. "Choose today whom you will serve. Do not follow other gods. As for me and my house, we will serve the Lord."

In generations to come, when Israel followed these words, God's people enjoyed a fruitful life. But, when they did not, Israel suffered horrible consequences for their sin.

The crowd answered, "We will never leave the Lord. We will always love Him. He is our God."

But Joshua said to the people, "You are not able to serve the Lord. He is a holy God. He is a jealous God. He will not forgive your sins. If you turn from God and serve other gods, He will destroy you."

And the people replied, "No, we will serve and obey the Lord."

So Joshua made a covenant with the people that day and wrote these words in the Book of the Law. He also placed a stone near the sanctuary of the Lord: a seventh, and final, stone to help Israel remember God's promises.

After all of this, Joshua died. He was 110 years old and was buried in the hill country of Ephraim along with the bones of Joseph, which Israel had carried up from Egypt at Shechem.

Israel served the Lord all the days of Joshua and all the days of the elders who outlived Joshua.

At the end of his life, Joshua's words were truer than even he probably knew. Remember, Joshua said, "You are not able to serve the Lord...He will not forgive your sins."

Joshua was right. But because of Jesus, these words can instead read, "You are not able to serve the Lord...but He *will* forgive your sins."

Here's what I mean....

Our sin leads us to serve ourselves instead of the Lord. It is a terrible mess when we disobey the Lord and seek our own pleasure outside of God's law.

Our sin is a big deal. It is selfish, harmful, and does not honor God. Throughout the Bible, God says He will not leave the guilty unpunished. He has to punish sin in order to forgive sin because He is a God of justice.

But the good news of the gospel is that we do not receive the punishment that our sins deserve. Instead, God's own Son, Jesus, received what we deserve.

Jesus is the only one who served God perfectly and never sinned, so He is the only one who could offer Himself as a spotless sacrifice to die in our place. If we hate our sin, turn from it, and have faith in Jesus, our sin is forgiven because of God's kindness to us through His Son.

Maybe you have trusted Jesus in this way before. If so, I hope this book has helped you to know more about our wonderful God.

Maybe you are making some connections for the first time. You are discovering that you stand guilty before God, just like every other person in history...including those we just met in Joshua.

But, if you trust that Jesus has died the death your sins deserve, then you can begin to live in response to the love God has for you!

Instead of the stones in Joshua that reminded people of God's faithfulness, your life can become a witness to God's faithfulness! You become like a living stone that is built together with other believers on the foundation of Jesus Christ, the cornerstone (see 1 Peter 2).

Because of what Jesus did, forgiving us and making us part of this family, we get to live the life He deserves...not in the Promised Land, but forever in heaven with the One who made us and loves us more than we could ever know.